STEIN FOLLI

Secret to Success

To you seeking success

If you can dream it, you can do it.

— Walt Disney

Contents

Acknowledgement

We thank the anonymous believers who have continued to spread the message of this book.

I

Success

Success is the sum of small efforts repeated day in and day out.

— Robert Collier

Introduction

You may have had to venture into one thing or the other at different points in your life. It could be as simple as getting a household item fixed to getting a college degree or even starting and running a business. You may have succeeded in some, and failed in others.

The difference between a person who has surpassed all obstacles and seen an idea through to its completion and another who was only able to achieve wishful thinking with any chance of seeing it to the end is what I refer to as success.

If we pick ten successful folks out there, you would be surprised to know that they have all at one point thought about quitting. Success isn't something that is given on a platter of gold; it's a process, a deliberate journey aimed at achieving a goal.

Let us take a quick look at these two characters:

Mr. A had always dreamt about attending Cambridge University. After high school, despite knowing that he didn't have enough to sponsor himself, he still didn't relent. He worked odd jobs and kept on applying for scholarships. He was denied admission twice. He persisted, and today, Mr. A got not only that most sought after Cambridge certificate, but he also came out top of his class.

Mr. B also had the same dream, but he put in very little effort. He only wished he got admitted into the institution; he took no conscious steps. He applied once, got rejected and quit applying for admission. All his dreams were nothing but wishes because he did not attempt to actualize his vision. Mr. B felt like Cambridge was a far cry from what he could achieve and didn't even bother putting in much effort.

What the two scenarios are telling us is that success doesn't come easily, and it's not something handed over to us. Success is something you earn. It might start from being a wish, successive baby steps, pitfalls, and setbacks here and there until the goal is finally achieved. What distinguishes success and failure is that determination to pull through to the end. Successful people from different walks of life will tell you that success comes from the firm resolve not to let go even when it appears impossible.

This book is written to give you a broader understanding of success, what it is, steps required to achieve it, and how to stay successful in every area of your life.

What is Success

Many people and books have defined success in relation to their subjectivity. Interestingly, most of these definitions have a reoccurring theme. But for us to fully understand the concept, let us look at some of these definitions:

- Success can be seen as the achievement of something that you planned to do or attempted to do. It can be a plan or an attempt that achieves good results.

- Success is 1% inspiration, 97% perspiration and 2% attention to details. Success is a combination of small habits, a tenacious spirit, and a lot of luck.

- Success is the link between the conception of an idea and the actualization of the idea.

- Success is the constant effort geared towards the completion of a task.

The definitions above are just a minute quarter of what success entails, but these definitions could best sum up the essence of this book. Let us take a look at each of the definitions:

The first one describes success as the achievement of something that you planned to do. This can be said to be the sum up of the whole concept of success. It isn't something that you plan to do. It's not something that you think about or something you feel you want to do. Instead, it is something that you end up achieving. What this is telling us is that success doesn't come if you do not carry out your plans. It takes effort to turn your ideas into success.

The second one is closely knitted to the first; It explains that the first step to success is that inspiration to do something differently. It is this inspiration that is then watered with perspiration, which takes the bulk of the cycle. Without perspiration, your inspiration cannot get the push that it needs to scale through.

You need to work very hard such that your idea doesn't die a natural death. The next in line is the attention that you need to pay to details. This attention would include knowing when to take a break, knowing when to push harder, and so on.

The third definition summarizes everything by showing us that all the elements work hand in hand. It also explains that luck plays an important role in the whole success process. It is equally important to understand that without effort, there is no luck.

The fourth is almost a repetition of the second definition. It also states that the actualization of an idea is more important than the initial conceptualization. Don't just have a plan; you need to work consistently towards achieving it.

Now that we have attempted defining the concept, the next step would be to examine what the steps towards achieving success are:

Steps towards Success

THE IDEA- There is no successful person in the world who didn't have a reason that made want to be successful. It could be for the fear or experience of poverty that would make you think about starting a business.

Someone could be bent on getting educated because his/her parents couldn't get gainful employment because they were not educated. I could decide to start a non-governmental organization focusing on healthcare delivery to infants because I want to solve the problem of maternal and infant mortality.

What the aforementioned tells us is that there is no success without the conceptualization of an idea. There must be something that you want to work towards actualizing.

THE RESOLVE- An idea will remain nothing but the idea that it is until there is that inspiration to push it. There is no successful person out there today who would say that they sat in the comfort of their home and their idea miraculously metamorphosed into a final product.

It takes that inner will, the strength, and the firm belief that what you want to achieve will pull through.

SET REALISTIC TARGETS- After the resolve to turn your ideas into success, the next thing needed is to establish a target. It is vital to set goals that you can achieve at every point of the way.

Imagine a person that wants to become a bestselling author; you don't just wake up and attain that position. You must have prepared for long nights of writing, rewriting, and editing rough drafts of your work. By doing this, you are setting the pace for that which you want to become.

DEVELOP A THICK SKIN- You need to understand that success takes constant and conscious efforts. There will down moments, no doubt about that but what should be your inspiration is that ultimate goal that you have in mind- which is to become successful.

Imagine the number of rejection letters a scholarship applicant faces before the last email that changes the whole narrative comes in. Have you heard about the number of times contestants on "Americas Got talent" entered for the competition or the number of rejections they received?

To be successful in life, you need to be so thick-skinned that nothing distracts you on the way. You take rejections as a means to strategizing and figuring out where you got it wrong or what needs to be improved upon.

BE FOCUSED- To become successful in life, you need to be very focused on that which you set to achieve. Tongues will wag, not everyone will support you, but that should not deter you from the end result that you wish for. Successful people know what they want, and they stick to it even when it appears like they are not making good sense.

HAVE CONSTANT REEVALUATION- Do not get too overwhelmed on the journey to becoming successful that you forget to check if you are still doing the right thing. Most times, people tend to get lost in the crowd because they fail to check themselves. You might be lucky enough to still hit the success bar, but most people tend to lose it at that stage just because of the failure to evaluate the targets that they set towards achieving their goals.

Reevaluating yourself will help you to determine that which you have done right or wrong, things that you need to celebrate yourself for and so on. We know failure works hand in hand with being successful, but reevaluations make it possible for us to understand how to forge ahead.

II

Secret

The price of success is hard work
— Vince Lombardi

Secrets

Mike Bloomberg is a billionaire and a former mayor of New York City. He credited long hours of work to his success, but something else he revealed was one of the secondary benefits of working long hours at the office; the only people there are successful.

If we take a look at Mike Bloomberg's story, you will realize that all we've been saying about being successful is true. There are certain things that should be put into place in order to attain success. Let us take a look at some of the common secrets.

1. Never stay in your comfort zone. If you stay in your comfort zone, no significant changes will happen in your life.

2. Cultivate the habit of not giving up. Most times, things don't work out the first time it is attempted. Remember when you learnt to ride a bike. Did you get it right on the first attempt?

3. Set your eyes and heart on the end goal. Stay focused until you get to the finish line. Remember that old saying, "As you think, so shall you be."

4. Every journey begins with a step. Conquer your challenges one day

at a time. Deal with difficulties as they arise and you will be one step closer to becoming successful.

5. Keep moving forward. Never stop investing in acquiring more knowledge. The moment you stop improving, the sooner you start to decline.

Make it your goal to become better every day. The Japanese concept of Kaizen posits that minor daily improvements eventually result in huge advantages.

6. When you're ready to quit, you're closer than you think. There's an old Chinese saying: "The temptation to quit will be greatest just before you are about to succeed."

Consistency

If you have been following me on this journey, you must have figured out by now that there is a recurring theme in becoming successful. That is the fact that you need to be consistent in whatever you do. Success is not handed out to those who give up after the first attempt; rather, it is for those who do not give up.

We need to be consistent because, without it, you'll never finish. The Key is Consistency. Failure will come, sometimes more than once. You will be disappointed and feel defeated. But with a constancy of purpose, you will definitely reach the finish line.

• Consistency In Action

Consistency-in-action doesn't mean that you keep repeating the same thing over and over again. It's about growing, developing, and learning how to make more of what you're doing better. Adapting new ideas into your work and being creative in what you do.

Conclusion

Let us have a summary of all that we have explored in the course of this book:

1. Expect something wonderful to happen every day.
2. Focus on what you're doing now rather than the results.

Keep other opportunities in reserve so you can quickly move on.

1. Create goals that motivate you to achieve something possible.
2. Ask questions rather than providing answers
3. Measure what's truly relevant.
4. Take responsibility for your low performers.
5. Keep track of how you spend time; that's half the battle.
6. Prioritize based on what accomplishes the most with the least effort.
7. Remember, consistency is the key.